Please color in this book. When I was littl
I didn't always color in the righ
Mama didn't like it when I ruined a good book.
This book is made especially for you to color any way you wish.

SPOT

**Let Spot be your guide.
He will introduce you to the vowel "O".
Spot has a full Kit of Tools for you to use.
He will help you learn to read
as you use this Tool Kit.**

1

MASTERY TOOL

Directions: Have the student say each word part. Use the short sound of the vowel.
Add the letter 'T' in each blank.
Go back down the list and say the whole word you just made.
Notice that these words all end with the same sound. We call these words 'rhyming' words.

blo__

co__

clo__

do__

go__

ho__

jo__

lo__

no__

po__

plo__

The short "O" sound opens your
mouth and drops your jaw
all the way down.

ro__

slo__

Spo__

to__

tro__

MASTERY TOOL

Directions: Have the student say each word part. Use the short sound of the vowel.
Add the letter 'B' in each blank.
Go back down the list and say the whole word you just made.
Notice that these words all end with the same sound. We call these words 'rhyming' words.

The short "O" sound opens your
mouth and drops your jaw
all the way down.

jo__
kno__
lo__
mo__
ro__
so__
glo__
slo__

Bo__
co__
do__
fo__
go__
ho__

MASTERY TOOL

SEEING DIFFERENCES

Directions:
Say each word.
In each box, put an **X** on the word that does not match.

Spot Spot Stop	jot jot tot
cot sot cot	lot not lot
dot hot dot	rot not not
lot got got	pot pot got
hot hot not	dot rot rot

MASTERY TOOL

RECOGNIZING CAPITAL LETTERS

Directions:
Say each word.
Draw a line between words that belong together.

See ———————— see

be   We

he   oh

Me   Go

we   Be

Oh   me

go   so

no   No

So   He

Welcome to your first COLOR BOOK READER.
Color the pictures as you learn to read.
Use the colors you like to make this your very own book.

Chapter 1

SPOT

See Spot.

See Spot.
Oh, Spot!
Oh, oh, oh!

Oh, Spot!
See Spot.
Spot is hot.

Oh, Spot! Oh!
Spot is hot.
Go Spot! Go!

Go, go, go!
See Spot go.
Go Spot! Go!
Spot is hot.

**Oh, Spot! Go!
See Spot go.
Spot is not hot.**

Come Spot!
Come Spot! Come!
Come, come, come!

Come Spot! Come!
See Spot come.
Oh, oh, oh!
Spot is not hot.

Come Spot! Come!
Come, come, come.
See Spot.
Spot is not hot.

Oh, oh, oh!
No, Spot! No!
No, no, no!

Go, go, go!
Go Spot! Go!
Oh, oh, oh!

MASTERY TOOL

COMPREHENSION

Directions:
Circle the best answer.

page 7

Is Spot happy?
Yes   No

Why is Spot sad?
Cold   Hot

page 14

Is Spot happy?
Yes   No

Is Spot hot?
Yes   No

page 15

What did Spot do?
Come   Go

Did Spot come?
Yes   No

MASTERY TOOL

COMPREHENSION

Directions:
Circle the best answer.
Write the best word in the blank.

page 16

Is Spot wet?
Yes   No

Did Donny get wet?
Yes   No

Is Donny happy?
Yes   No

Is Spot hot?
Yes   No

page 17

Donny tells Spot to _____.
Come   Go

_____ Spot! Go!
Go   Come

19

MASTERY TOOL

24 Rhyming Words to Read

Directions: Your child is learning how to use a new tool. Give them all the encouragement they need. As your child reads down this list of rhyming words, you may need to give hints that will help them pronounce each word correctly.
There are many words in this list. Don't try to read them all at once.
Move on to the next chapter after your child is comfortable with these words.

be	blot	not
he	clot	plot
me	cot	pot
see	dot	rot
tee	got	slot
we	hot	sot
ye	jot	Spot
	lot	tot
		trot

MASTERY TOOL

22 More Rhyming Words to Read

Bob	job	come	go
cob	knob	some	no
dob	lob		oh
fob	mob		so
glob	rob	his	
gob	slob	is	
hob	sob		

MASTERY TOOL

27 Spelling Words in ABC Order

Directions:
1. Call out words from this list.
2. Have your child write them down.
3. Give hints to help your child see how the word is spelled.
4. This is a long list, so go at it in bits and pieces. Don't try to have your child spell all these words at once.
5. You can come back another day and learn to spell more words.

be	fob	is
blot	glob	job
Bob	go	jot
clot	gob	knob
cob	got	lob
come	he	lot
cot	his	me
dob	hob	mob
dot	hot	no

MASTERY TOOL

19 More Spelling Words in ABC Order

not	sob
oh	some
plot	sot
pot	Spot
rob	stop
rot	tee
see	tot
slob	trot
slot	we
so	

MASTERY TOOL

Directions: Have the student say each word part. Use the short sound of the vowel.
Add the letter 'M' in each blank.
Go back down the list and say the whole word you just made.
Notice that these words all end with the same sound. We call these words 'rhyming' words.

fro__

Mo__

po__

pro__

To__

The short "O" sound opens your
mouth and drops your jaw
all the way down.

MASTERY TOOL

RECOGNIZING CAPITAL LETTERS

Directions:
Say each word.
Draw a line between words that belong together.

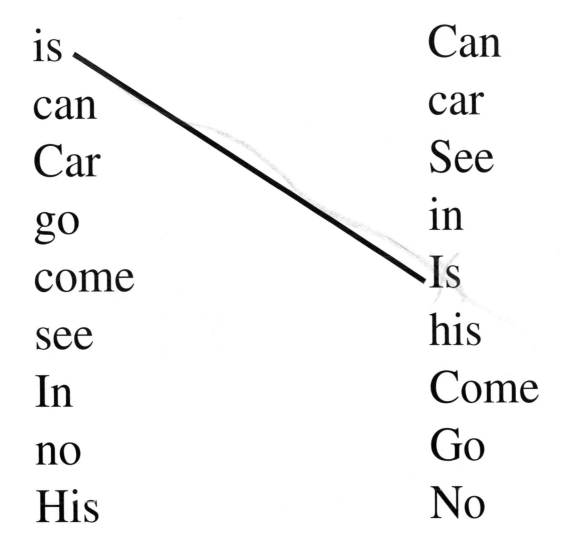

is	Can
can	car
Car	See
go	in
come	Is
see	his
In	Come
no	Go
His	No

Chapter 2

FATHER

See Father.
Oh! Oh!
See Father.

See Father go.
Go Father! Go!
Go, go, go!

See Donny go.
Donny can go.

See Donny.
Oh, see Donny!
See Donny go.

Go Donny! Go!
See Donny go.
Go, go, go!

No, Spot!
No, Spot! No!
Spot can not go.

Father can go.
Donny can go.
Spot can not go.

MASTERY TOOL

COMPREHENSION

Directions:
Circle the best answer.
Write the best word in the blank.

page 27

Did Father go in the car?
Yes   No

Father can go in the ____.
car   box

page 30

Will Donny go?
Yes   No

Donny will go in the ___.
box   car

page 32

Did Spot go in the car?
Yes   No

Is Spot happy?
Yes   No

MASTERY TOOL

19 Rhyming Words to Read

Directions: Your child is learning how to use a new tool. Give them all the encouragement they need. As your child reads down this list of rhyming words, you may need to give hints that will help them pronounce each word correctly.
There are many words in this list. Don't try to read them all at once.
Move on to the next chapter after your child is comfortable with these words.

Father	**an**	**man**
bother	**ban**	**Nan**
	can	**pan**
	Dan	**ran**
Donny	**fan**	**tan**
Bonny	**Jan**	**van**
Johnny		
Lonny		
Ronny		

MASTERY TOOL

19 Spelling Words in ABC Order

Directions:
1. Call out words from this list.
2. Have your child write them down.
3. Give hints to help your child see how the word is spelled.
4. This is a long list, so go at it in bits and pieces. Don't try to have your child spell all these words at once.
5. You can come back another day and learn to spell more words.

an	fan	pan
ban	Father	ran
Bonny	Jan	Ronny
bother	Johnny	tan
can	Lonny	van
Dan	man	
Donny	Nan	

MASTERY TOOL

Directions: Have the student say each word part. Use the short sound of the vowel.
Add the letter 'G' in each blank.
Go back down the list and say the whole word you just made.
Notice that these words all end with the same sound. We call these words 'rhyming' words.

bo__

co__

clo__

do__

fo__

flo__

fro__

go__

gro__

ho__

jo__

no__

so__

slo__

to__

The short "O" sound opens your
mouth and drops your jaw
all the way down.

MASTERY TOOL

FOLLOWING DIRECTIONS

1. Write your name above Spot.

2. Color his hair brown.

3. Color his bib blue.

4. Draw a line from Spot to his house.

5. Color Spot's house red.

6. Write SPOT under his house.

7. Color the bird house green.

8. Color the nest yellow.

9. Color the log orange.

MASTERY TOOL

SEEING DIFFERENCES

Directions:
Say each word.
In each box, put an **X** on the word that does not match.

is his is	is in in
car can can	his his this
stop drop stop	not rot not
and and sand	far car car
Go So Go	box box fox

Chapter 3

CAR

See the car.
See the car.
Go car! Go!

See the car go.
Go car! Go!
The car can go and go!

See Donny go.
See the car go.
See Donny go in the car.

Father can go.
See Father go.
See the car go.
See Father go in the car.

See the car go.
Father can go.
Donny can go.
See Father and Donny go.

Oh, oh, oh!
The car can not go.
No, no, no!

Stop Father! Stop!
See the car stop.
The car can not go.
Stop, stop, stop!

The car can not go.
Oh, oh, oh!
See the car.

See the car.
The car can not go.
No! No!
The car can not go.

See Father.
See the car.
The car can not go.

The car can go.
Go car! Go!
Go, go, go!

MASTERY TOOL

COMPREHENSION

Fill in the blanks.

page 41

See the _____.

box   car

Go! Car! _____!

Go   the

page 42

_____ the car go.

Donny   See

The car _____ go.

car   can

page 43

See _____ go.

the   Donny

Go in _____ car.

can   the

MASTERY TOOL

COMPREHENSION

Directions:
Circle the best answer.
Write the best word in the blank.

page 47 Can the car go?
Yes   No

Stop Father! _____!
Go   Stop

page 49 The car can go.
Yes   No

Donny will go in the ____.
box   car

page 51 Can the car go?
Yes   No

Father is _____.
happy   sad

MASTERY TOOL

46 Rhyming Words to Read

Directions: Your child is learning how to use a new tool. Give them all the encouragement they need. As your child reads down this list of rhyming words, you may need to give hints that will help them pronounce each word correctly.
There are many words in this list. Don't try to read them all at once.
Move on to the next chapter after your child is comfortable with these words.

and	sand	bin	she	flog
band	stand	din	the	frog
bland	strand	fin	three	gog
brand		gin	tree	grog
gland	bar	in		hog
grand	car	kin	bog	jog
hand	far	pin	cog	nog
land	jar	sin	clog	sog
	par	tin	dog	slog
	tar	win	fog	tog

MASTERY TOOL

48 Spelling Words in ABC Order

Directions:
1. Call out words from this list.
2. Have your child write them down.
3. Give hints to help your child see how the word is spelled.
4. This is a long list, so go at it in bits and pieces. Don't try to have your child spell all these words at once.
5. You can come back another day and learn to spell more words.

and	din	grand	par	strand
band	dog	grog	pin	tar
bar	far	hand	sand	the
bin	fin	hog	she	this
bland	flog	in	sin	three
bog	fog	jar	slog	tin
brand	frog	jog	sog	tog
car	gin	kin	stand	tree
clog	gland	land	stop	win
cog	gog	nog		

MASTERY TOOL

Directions: Have the student say each word part. Use the short sound of the vowel.
Add the letter 'D' in each blank.
Go back down the list and say the whole word you just made.
Notice that these words all end with the same sound. We call these words 'rhyming' words.

The short "O" sound opens your
mouth and drops your jaw
all the way down.

co___

clo___

Go___   pro___

ho___   ro___

mo___   so___

no___   To___

po___   tro___

MASTERY TOOL

SEEING DIFFERENCES

Directions:
Say each word.
In each box, put an **X** on the word that does not match.

Jack Jack Zack	pop hop pop
box fox box	in pin in
hot hot got	pot not not
lot got got	and and land
mop top mop	see the see
ran ran man	be be he

MASTERY TOOL

RECOGNIZING CAPITAL LETTERS

Directions:
Say each word.
Draw a line between words that belong together.

Mother   In

stop   jack

in   mother

Jack   Is

box   Stop

Donny   And

car   Box

is   Car

and   donny

57

Chapter 4

BOX

See the box.

Donny sees the box.

Oh, see the box!

See the box.
Donny sees the box.
Is the box for Donny?

Donny sees the box.
The box is for Donny.
See the box for Donny.
The box is for Donny.

What is in the box?
The box is for Donny.
Oh, oh!
What is in the box?

See the box.
What is in the box?
See, see, see!

Oh, oh, oh!
See Jack!
See Jack pop.
See Jack.

Pop Jack! Pop!
See Jack pop.
See Jack in a box.
Pop, pop, pop!

MASTERY TOOL

COMPREHENSION

Directions:
Circle the best answer.
Write the best word in the blank.

Today is Donny's birthday.

Donny is _____.
hot   sad   happy   page 59

What is in the box?   page 61
Jack   Spot   Jim

Color Jack's hair red.   page 64

Color Jack's body green.

MASTERY TOOL

21 Rhyming Words to Read

Directions: Your child is learning how to use a new tool. Give them all the encouragement they need. As your child reads down this list of rhyming words, you may need to give hints that will help them pronounce each word correctly.
There are many words in this list. Don't try to read them all at once.
Move on to the next chapter after your child is comfortable with these words.

box	cod	pod
fox	clod	prod
lox	God	rod
pox	hod	sod
sox	mod	Tod
	nod	trod

back

Jack

sack

Zack

MASTERY TOOL

27 Spelling Words in ABC Order

Directions:
1. Call out words from this list.
2. Have your child write them down.
3. Give hints to help your child see how the word is spelled.
4. This is a long list, so go at it in bits and pieces. Don't try to have your child spell all these words at once.
5. You can come back another day and learn to spell more words.

a	Jack	rod
back	lox	sack
box	mod	sees
clod	Mother	sod
cod	nod	sox
for	pod	Tod
fox	pop	trod
God	pox	what
hod	prod	Zack

MASTERY TOOL

Directions: Have the student say each word part. Use the short sound of the vowel.
Add the letter 'P' in each blank.
Go back down the list and say the whole word you just made.
Notice that these words all end with the same sound. We call these words 'rhyming' words.

bo__	lo__
co__	mo__
clo__	po__
cro__	pro__
dro__	slo__
fo__	so__
flo__	sto__
ho__	to__

The short "O" sound opens your
mouth and drops your jaw
all the way down.

MASTERY TOOL

Directions: Have the student say each word part. Use the short sound of the vowel.
Add the letters 'ck' in each blank.
Go back down the list and say the whole word you just made.
Notice that these words all end with the same sound. We call these words 'rhyming' words.

The short "O" sound opens your
mouth and drops your jaw
all the way down.

blo___

clo___

do___

ho___

kno___

lo___

mo___

ro___

so___

smo___

to___

Chapter 5

JACK

See Jack!
See the can.
See, see!

See the can.
Jack sees the can.
What is in the can?

Jack sees the can.
The can is not hot.
What is in the can?

Come Father!
Come and see.
See the can.
What is in the can?

Is the can for Jack?
No Jack! No!
The can is not for Jack.

FATHER AND JACK

Chapter 6

**See Father.
The can is for Father.
Father is hot.**

The can is not hot.
Father can pop the top.
The can is for Father.

Pop the top, Father.
See Father and the can.
Father is hot.

See Jack.
See Jack and the can.
See Father and Jack.

Father and Jack.
Father and Jack have cans.

The can is for Father.
Father is hot.
The can is for Jack.
Jack is hot.

See the can.
Father is not hot.
Jack is not hot.

MASTERY TOOL

FOLOWING DIRECTIONS

Directions:
After reading each sentence, draw a line to the best picture.

page 77

Jack wants a can.

Father wants a can.

page 74

Father and Jack are happy.

1. Color two cans red.

2. Color two cans blue.

3. Color the tree trunks brown.

page 76

4. Color Jack's feet yellow.

5. Color Father's shirt green.

6. Write your name on Jack's beak.

MASTERY TOOL

28 Rhyming Words to Read

Directions: Your child is learning how to use a new tool. Give them all the encouragement they need. As your child reads down this list of rhyming words, you may need to give hints that will help them pronounce each word correctly.
There are many words in this list. Don't try to read them all at once.
Move on to the next chapter after your child is comfortable with these words.

bop	mop	block	mock
cop	pop	clock	rock
clop	plop	dock	sock
crop	prop	hock	smock
drop	slop	knock	tock
fop	sop	lock	
flop	stop		
hop	top		
lop			

MASTERY TOOL

30 Spelling Words in ABC Order

Directions:
1. Call out words from this list.
2. Have your child write them down.
3. Give hints to help your child see how the word is spelled.
4. This is a long list, so go at it in bits and pieces. Don't try to have your child spell all these words at once.
5. You can come back another day and learn to spell more words.

block	fop	pop
bop	have	prop
cans	hock	rock
clock	hop	slop
clop	knock	smock
cop	lock	sock
crop	lop	sop
dock	mock	stop
drop	mop	tock
flop	plop	top

Chapter 7

JACK AND SPOT

See Spot.

Oh, Spot!
See Spot.

See Jack.

No! Jack!
No, no, no!
See Spot.

Oh, Spot! Oh!
No, Jack!

Stop!
Stop Jack! Stop!
No, no, no!

See Spot go.
No, Jack! No!
Go, go, go!

MASTERY TOOL

SEEING DIFFERENCES

Directions:
Say each word.
In each box, put an **X** on the word that does not match.

and and said	is in is
box box fox	on no no
fan can can	not hot not
car can car	pop pop pot
go go got	see she see
not hot hot	stop stop spot

MASTERY TOOL

FOLLOWING DIRECTIONS

Directions: Match each picture with a word. Draw a line to the right word.

LOCK

LOGS

COT

MOP

SOCK

POT

Chapter 8

BOXES

Come Mother!
Come and see.
See the car.

See the car.
See the boxes.
Come and see.

See the box.
See in the box.
See, see, see!

What is for Donny?
See in the box.
What is for Donny?

Oh, see!
Donny can see.
Mother can see.
See what is for Donny.

Boxes, boxes.
See the boxes

Boxes, boxes.
Oh, boxes!
Boxes, boxes.

Oh, boxes!
See the boxes.

Oh, Mother!
See a box.

Oh, see a box!

See a box.
What is in the box?

Oh, oh, oh!

Mother sees a box.
What is in the box?
Boxes, boxes, boxes.

MASTERY TOOL

FOLLOWING DIRECTIONS

Directions:
Follow the directions.
Write the word in the blank.

page 103

How many boxes are in the picture? _____

Write your name on the biggest box.

Color one box yellow.

Color one box blue.

Color one box brown.

MASTERY TOOL

200 Words In Alphabetical Order

Your son or daughter now has all these words they can read and spell. I'm proud of you! You are both doing a great job! Congratulations! This is a list of all the words you have learned in Tool Kit #1. You are now ready to move on to Tool Kit #2. You are a success! Just look at all the words you already know!

a	blot	brand	cob
an	Bob	can	cod
and	bog	car	cog
back	bon	chock	come
ban	bong	chomp	cop
band	Bonny	chop	cot
bar	bop	clock	crop
be	boss	clod	Dan
bin	botch	clog	din
bland	bother	clop	dob
block	box	clot	dock

MASTERY TOOL

Alphabetical Word List Continued

doff	flop	go	hob
dog	fob	gob	hock
dong	fog	God	hod
Donny	fond	gog	hog
dot	fop	gong	hop
drop	for	got	hot
fan	fox	grand	in
far	frog	grog	is
Father	gin	hand	Jack
fin	gland	he	Jan
flog	glob	his	jar

MASTERY TOOL

Alphabetical Word List Continued

job	lock	lots	Mother
jog	loft	lox	Nan
Johnny	log	man	no
josh	logs	me	nod
jot	Lon	mob	nog
kin	long	mock	non
knob	Lonny	mod	not
knock	lop	mom	notch
land	lost	mop	off
lob	lot	moss	oh

Alphabetical Word List Continued

pan	prop	sees	slot
par	ran	she	smock
pin	rob	shock	so
plop	rock	shod	sob
plot	rod	shop	sock
pod	Ronny	shot	sod
pop	rot	sin	soft
pot	sack	slob	sog
pox	sand	slog	some
prod	see	slop	song

Alphabetical Word List Continued

sop	the	toss	ye
sot	this	tot	Zack
sox	thong	tree	
Spot	three	trod	
stand	tin	trot	
stop	tock	van	
strand	Tod	von	
tan	tog	we	
tar	Tom	what	
tee	top	win	